Book Design: Maggie Saleeb

ST SHENOUDA PRESS
8419 Putty Rd,
Putty, NSW, 2330
Sydney, Australia

www.stshenoudapress.com

ISBN: 978-0-6482814-2-9

SAINT SHENOUDA PRESS

All my life I have been looking after these sheep. I love them dearly. The problem is that there are now too many sheep, and I am getting old. I need a young shepherd boy. Maybe I can ask Shenouda's parents for his help!

"I'll watch over your son very well as he helps me with your sheep in the field," I said to Shenouda's parents.

"If you need it, you can also keep some of my wages in exchange for his help. I know that it isn't much, but it will help your family a little. And besides, I'm sure I will enjoy Shenouda's company. He seems like a nice Christian boy."

Shenouda's father replied, "Certainly! We both agree that to have Shenouda trained as a shepherd, the profession of many saints, is a worthy plan. Our young boy has grown into such a fine Christian and we would love to see him continue to mature."

"We'll miss Shenouda very much," said his mother in a worried voice. "But if you promise us that you will send him back each evening when the day's work is finished, then we agree to have him work with you."

"He is indeed our only son but we trust you with him," Shenouda's father added.

"Well then, consider it settled. Shenouda can come with me today," I eagerly replied.

Just in case they were still concerned, I further said, "Don't worry, I will send him back to you before the sun sets every day. I will teach him everything there is to know about being a shepherd, including all the knowledge passed down to me from my father."

Shenouda's parents were assured by my words and so gave their blessings before I took their son up into the fields. There I began training him how to become a shepherd.

"How do you train the sheep to listen to you?" Shenouda asked me.

"It's simple Shenouda. All you have to do is treat them with love and care. I hold both a rod and a staff in my hand. The sheep recognise the staff I hold as I walk and so they follow me wherever I go. As for the rod, I use it to strike any wild animals that try to attack the sheep."

Not only was it nice having him assist me in the field, it was also great to have someone to spend time with. When evening came, I honoured his parents' request and sent Shenouda down the hill to the village.

To my surprise, his parents came to me a few days later.

"Why haven't you been sending our son home on time as you promised?" Shenouda's father strongly asked.

"I have been so worried! Every time he wouldn't come home before sunset, I would think something bad had happened to him!" Shenouda's mother said in support of her husband. "We trusted you and made an agreement. How could you disappoint us like this?"

I assured them that I had indeed been sending Shenouda home before sunset each evening. I decided to speak to him about it.

"Shenouda, what did you think of the last few days working as a shepherd?" I asked him.

"It has been beautiful! I am enjoying it very much. It helped me understand why King David says, 'The Lord is my Shepherd' in Psalm 22, which I memorised off by heart yesterday. Just like we look after the sheep, the Lord also looks after us in the same way." Shenouda replied.

I admired his response, but I still did not find out why he has been arriving home late.

"What do you do when you go home Shenouda?"

"I pray and thank God."

This again did not yet explain to me why he does not go straight home.

The following night before sunset, I decided to follow Shenouda. I had to find out why he was not going home on time. I kept my distance from him, so that he could not see me following. I was close enough though to still manage to keep my eyes on him. I hid behind a large tree and watched the boy.

To my amazement, he walked right into a lake.

I then heard him speaking, but I could not see anyone else around... he was praying! He had his arms outstretched toward the sky and was saying,

"Oh my dear Lord, let me follow in your path."

It made sense now. He prays at the lake before going home!

The next time I saw his parents, I told them everything.

"I saw your young boy in the lake with his arms raised in prayers to God. And you know what? I saw his fingers shining like flaming candles! Perhaps he is spending time at the lake in prayer each night, and that is why he does not come home on time," I explained to them.

"Thank you for finding this out! Although we are upset that he did not tell us, we are proud of his love for God." Shenouda's mother replied.

Although I needed Shenouda's help with the sheep, I felt like God had another plan for this boy. So, I continued telling his parents,

"Besides, I am not worthy to have him stay with me. He has a strong relationship with the Lord. He talks to Him, and the Lord in turn lights up his hands with the Holy Spirit. I saw it with my own eyes. It is best that I continue to shepherd your flock alone. The boy knows God and he must follow His will."

So Shenouda's parents took him home.

After a number of months, his father came to check on his sheep in the field. "How is Shenouda?" I asked.

9

His father told me all about what had happened to him.

"When Shenouda turned nine years old, my brother-in-law, Abba Pigol, invited us to his monastery, called the White Monastery. Abba Pigol described a vision he had that Shenouda would someday become a monk! He kept Shenouda with him, having him stay back with the other thirty monks.

My wife and I visit the monastery nearly every week. It is a small area but extremely beautiful! How joyful it is to see our son becoming a stronger Christian and to witness how much the other monks admire him!"

Several decades passed before I saw Shenouda's father again. On this visit in the year 385 AD, he told me about his son becoming a monk indeed, as Abba Pigol predicted, and how he spends his time training new monks.

I also heard that because Shenouda was so well-known and respected in Upper Egypt that St. Cyril the Great had invited him to join him at the Council of Ephesus. Shenouda was to help St. Cyril as he had a great zeal for the Orthodox faith.

St. Cyril was able to stop Nestorius from spreading false teachings about Jesus,

with the help of Abba Shenouda. For his punishment, Nestorius was sent away and his wrong teachings were stopped from spreading.

One day, Shenouda's father asked me to go to the market and sell the sheep that were getting old. I was thankfully able to sell the sheep at the market but then I overheard people talking about Shenouda. They said that he was ordained as the abbot, meaning he was put in charge of the other monks. They also mentioned that he put a pledge in place, which the new monks had to recite before joining the monastery.

The monks would live outside the monastery for a period of time first and then, if they were deemed worthy, they were let into the monastery and accepted as monks. Many, many people wanted to become monks.

Not only did he care for those in the monastery, but he also took care of all the believers in the surrounding villages.

He would invite them all to the monastery and study the bible with them and give them all that they needed. Abba Shenouda would also encourage the monks to use their talents to serve the local people.

Those who were doctors would check up on the sick and those who were teachers would teach the illiterate how to read. Many other services like this were organised by Abba Shenouda so that the monastery became an example of true Christian love.

Despite being so busy serving the people, Abba Shenouda always made sure that he spent a lot of time praying to God. He once spent three years in the desert alone, in prayer, when all of a sudden, he heard a heavenly voice saying, "Shenouda, you truly have become the leader of the monks."

There was much other activity in this monastery also. Besides the traditional roles of prayer and worship, and the usual tasks of rope and basket weaving, Abba Shenouda encouraged weaving and tailoring linen, cultivating flax, the working of leather and shoemaking, writing and bookbinding, carpentry, metal working, and pottery making.

He tried to encourage the monks to use their talents and skills for the service of the monastery. The monastery grew to cover a large area of land. All of the monks were required to learn to read and many of them learnt to write.

Abba Shenouda himself also wrote many things. He loved to write sermons and to quote the Holy Scripture, usually from memory, since he memorised a lot of bible verses when he was a young boy. His knowledge of the Coptic and Greek languages was very good and he read many of the writings and stories of the saints. He preferred to use the Coptic language though, to prevent people forgetting the language.

I began to wonder, how was a monastery of that enormous size even built? And where did the funds come from? I left the market and, on the way home, stopped by to see Abba Shenouda's parents. It was Shenouda's mother who shared the following story.

"The Lord Jesus Christ appeared to my son, Abba Shenouda, and told him that he should go into the desert. He was instructed by Him to pick up anything he saw on the way and use it for building the monastery. So he went into the desert in obedience and stayed there to pray overnight.

When he was leaving the desert the next morning, he found a small leather bag of silver coins, and realised this was sent from God for the building of the monastery. He used this money to pay the craftsmen, like the stonemasons and the carpenters, who would work on the church and expand the monastery.

The money was just enough to complete this great building." I decided to go and see the White Monastery which Abba Shenouda finished building.

I really wanted to see it. So one day, I packed some food and travelled there. I saw that the monastery had grown so much compared to its original small size.

There were now over four thousand monks and almost that many nuns too at a nearby monastery also built by Abba Shenouda! When I had entered, an elderly monk told me that Abba Shenouda was absent for a few days.

"He is not here, he is helping the people in the local villages. Abba Shenouda is a true leader, who is both brave and caring," the monk said. "Would you like me to show you around the monastery?"

"I would love to be shown around!" I replied.

"Look where we are now, we are standing inside the main church. In this church, Abba Shenouda invites all people to come and attend the vespers and midnight prayers every Saturday night. They then leave and come back Sunday morning for the Holy Liturgy. After the liturgy, everyone gets together on those tables beside the church to have a meal together."

"Wow! Sounds exciting! I'll make sure I come attend next Saturday!" I exclaimed.

"That would be great my son. Here, look outside to your right. That is the building in which the monks stay. Each monk has his own room.

We spend time in there individually, praying and reading the Bible, and then come out to meet the guests and do different jobs around the monastery.

We also attend a daily prayer together both early in the morning and at the end of the day." the monk continued. "This place is like Heaven!" I said with amazement.

The elderly monk also told me another wonderful story about Abba Shenouda. There was once a time when he tried to protect certain captives from the Barbarians. The Barbarians wanted to attack him and so raised their spears at him.

Abba Shenouda then signed the cross on them and quickly prayed. Immediately, their arms were frozen in the air and they could not move.

The king asked Abba Shenouda to pray that the soldiers' arms be healed. He, in return, freed the captives and brought them to the monastery and gave them food. Because of this act of kindness, many of them became Christians.

21

Some even asked that they stay at the monastery and become monks.

I was very impressed by everything I had both seen and heard during my visit to the monastery!

I then began the long journey home. My thoughts turned to a time long ago, when this young boy came to the hills to help me with the sheep.

I also remembered how I saw him worshipping God in the lake. I could not help but smile about how I was able to witness the growth of a young shepherd boy who later became a respected monk and a recognised saint.

At the age of 108, Abba Shenouda became very sick. Many think the illness was because of his old age. In pain, he called the monks to his bedside and asked them to sit in ordered ranks.

He cried out, "Behold the patriarchs have come with the prophets; behold the apostles with the bishops; behold the archimandrites have come with all the saints."

Then he asked them to take his hands so he could rise and worship the Lord. The room was filled with a wonderful fragrance as they lifted him up, and he said his final words, "God has come for me with his angels!"

The monks knew that Abba Shenouda had gone home with the Lord. They recalled that as a young shepherd, he had attended to a flock of sheep, but later on he instead became a shepherd that attended to the flock of Christ!

He began his life as an ordinary young boy, who loved God very much, and so ended his life as a glorious saint!

St. Shenouda the Archimandrite is honoured as a saint on the 7th day of the Coptic month of Abib on the 14th of July. This is the day that he gave up his soul to the Lord.

24

THE END